JAVᴀ

The Ultimate Beginner's Guide!

Table of Contents

Introduction

I want to thank you and congratulate you for purchasing this book...

"JAVA – The Ultimate Beginner's Guide"

Java – as the company behind it states – can be found in over three billion devices. Java is an *object-oriented* programming language that is similar to the *C#* language. Both are programming languages with high potential and a learning curve that beginners can become comfortable with in no time.

This book will cover the fundamental lessons of the Java programming language, which will be a beginner's gateway into the vast world of programming. Included are the following core topics:

- Understanding the Java program structure

- What are the Object-oriented Programming (OOP) and its key concepts

- Declaring and Working with Variables

- Getting to Know the Data Types

- Using Flow Control in a Java Program

- Importing other Classes (Random number generator & Scanner)

- Using Access Modifiers

- Learning about more Classes and Objects

- Using Constructors

- Understanding the Importance of Serialization

- Understanding Inheritance

- And Many More!

Thanks again for purchasing this book, I hope you enjoy it!

CHAPTER 1

How to Set up Java

Java was first introduced in the world in *1991* by *Sun Microsystems.* The people behind it were *Ed Frank, Mike Sheridan, Chris Warth, James Gosling,* and *Patrick Naughton.* Being an object-oriented language, it has the advantages of *reusability* when it comes to the written instructions, the focus on *data,* and the creation of *classes, objects* and *instances* that communicate through functions.

Chapter Overview:

***A Beginner's Introduction to the Java Programming Language*

***The Things you need to Get Started with Java*

***Setting up your Java Programming Environment for Free*

There are *4* main platforms of Java: *Java SE (Standard Edition), Java EE (Enterprise Edition, Java ME (Micro Edition),* and *JavaFX.* Java SE is for general computer applications and Java EE is added for web applications and servers. JavaFX is a multimedia platform (popularly known as *flash* players) with Java integration. Finally, Java ME is used mostly for *embedded systems* such as mobile phones and industrial control systems.

New to Programming?

If you are absolutely clueless in the exciting world of programming, then there are a few things you need to understand. First of all, you need an *Integrated Development Environment* specifically for Java before you can start writing codes. There are plenty of free IDEs on the internet that you can download. To get you started as quickly as possible, here are some of the most popular Java IDEs that beginners, hobbyists, and professionals use:

- **NetBeans** (https://netbeans.org) – NetBeans is a widely used IDE that is recommended as one of the best programming environments for beginners to the Java language. It is powerful and fast, and can support *all* Java platforms from SE to FX.

- **Eclipse** (www.eclipse.org) – Eclipse is one of the most popular Java IDEs that, like NetBeans, is open source and beginner-friendly. This IDE also has the best-looking interface with its responsive design and navigation.

- **BlueJ** (http://bluej.org/) – BlueJ is regarded as one of the best IDEs for beginners who want to learn their way around the Java programming language. In comparison to other IDEs on this list, BlueJ's interface is a lot simpler and is specifically designed to help a beginner understand the core concepts of Java programming.

- **DrJava** (www.drjava.org) – Last on this list is the lightweight IDE, *DrJava* that is also designed for new learners. Despite the simplicity of this IDE, it has a high ceiling and is powerful enough for adept programmers.

Naturally, the user interface, added features and support for each IDE will vary. However, the language itself remains exactly the same. However, for the sake of all the lessons throughout this book, the **NetBeans** IDE will be used. You may use the same IDE if you want the exact screenshots for each lesson, but remember that this is completely optional.

Finally, take note that if you are a student who is learning Java in school or any educational institution/organization, then the IDE should be supplied by your instructor.

The Java Development Kit

In addition to a Java IDE, your computer needs to have the *Java Development Kit* or *JDK* that acts as both a *compiler* and *interpreter*. Basically, a compiler translates written code into machine language. You can download the latest JDK version from *Oracle's* website here:

www.oracle.com/technetwork/java/javase/downloads/index.html

Be sure to download the appropriate version of JDK from this website. The download section should look like this:

Product / File Description	File Size	Download
Linux x86	146.9 MB	jdk-8u51-linux-i586.rpm
Linux x86	166.95 MB	jdk-8u51-linux-i586.tar.gz
Linux x64	145.19 MB	jdk-8u51-linux-x64.rpm
Linux x64	165.25 MB	jdk-8u51-linux-x64.tar.gz
Mac OS X x64	222.09 MB	jdk-8u51-macosx-x64.dmg
Solaris SPARC 64-bit (SVR4 package)	139.36 MB	jdk-8u51-solaris-sparcv9.tar.Z
Solaris SPARC 64-bit	98.8 MB	jdk-8u51-solaris-sparcv9.tar.gz
Solaris x64 (SVR4 package)	139.79 MB	jdk-8u51-solaris-x64.tar.Z
Solaris x64	96.45 MB	jdk-8u51-solaris-x64.tar.gz
Windows x86	176.02 MB	jdk-8u51-windows-i586.exe
Windows x64	180.51 MB	jdk-8u51-windows-x64.exe

If your computer has a *32-bit operating system,* download the matching system name affixed with *x86.* Otherwise, if you are using a *64-bit operating system,* download the one with *x64.* It is recommended for you to download the latest version of JDK from this website.

Java is NOT JavaScript

Before getting started, remember that *JavaScript* is not similar nor a part of Java. Unlike the Java platform used to create stand-alone applications and *applets,* JavaScript is a *scripting language* that is commonly integrated in web pages for functionality that cannot be achieved with simple HTML. If you want to learn JavaScript, then this is *not* the book for you.

CHAPTER 2

How to Write a Program with Java

After installing your chosen IDE and the latest JDK version, you can now get started with programming your first Java application but first, you need to understand the Java program structure, the main components of a Java program, and how they work together to create an application.

Chapter Overview:

**Introduction to Java Stand-alone Applications

**Introduction to Classes, Objects, and Instances

**The Main Parts of a Java Program (Statements, Declarations, and Methods)

The two primary software types you can create with Java are *applications* and *applets*. As what the name sounds like, applets are smaller applications (specifically just *pieces* of software code) that are run within a web browser, often used for interactivity and navigation enhancement. Unlike standalone applications written in Java, applets do not require an interpreter to be executed.

For the most part in this book, you will be learning how to code *console applications* that run in console environments. IDEs have built-in console environments for testing such programs. Learning with console operations is crucial in understanding the fundamentals of Java programming.

Classes, Objects and Instances

The utilization of **classes**, **objects**, and **instances** is what defines an object-oriented programming language. They are the sectors that make up a program, and the best way to understand them is to understand the relationship that exists between them:

- **Class** – The highest in the group is the *class*, which encompasses everything in object-oriented programming.

- **Object** – Objects apply the specifications set by classes. They are instances of a class.

- **Instance** – Finally, an *instance* can be the same as objects since they describe an *individual* instantiation.

In programming, *classes* set the definition for objects, but these specifications are not loaded into the computer's memory. Instead, they act as mere *blueprints;* ready to be used in case an object under that class is instantiated. There could be multiple copies or *instances* of an object or class throughout a program.

The best way to understand this as a beginner is to use layman's terms using real world examples. Let's say that *plant* is a class of immobile objects. A *tree* is an object under the *plant* class and the *willow tree* in your backyard is an instance of that object. At the same time, it is also an instance of the *tree* class, which is at the top of the hierarchy.

Your First Project

To start creating applications in Java, the first thing you need to do is to create an empty project from your IDE. Here are the specific steps on how to get started:

Creating an Empty Java SE Project

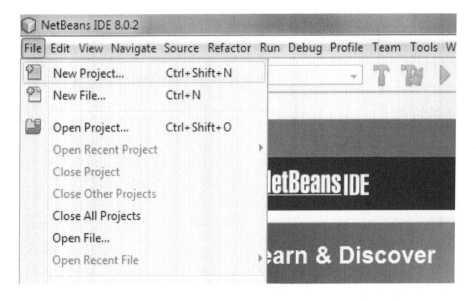

To create a new project, go to *File → New Project* (NetBeans shortcut: *Ctrl + Shift + N*).

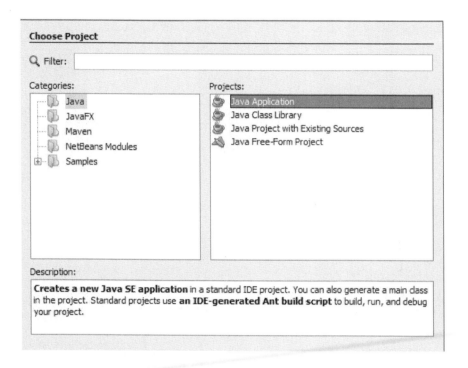

Under **Categories**, select *Java.* Choose *Java Application* on the right side – under **Projects.** Click *Next* to proceed to the **Name and Location** section.

Feel free to use names like *"My First Java App"* or *"My First Project"* when creating your project. Remember to use an appropriate name so you can use this project as reference later on. When applicable, set a specific location on your computer where your Java project will be saved. Doing so will allow you to locate your application without having to open it manually from your IDE.

What are Packages?

Source Packages are usually automatically created when creating a new project in most IDEs. In object-oriented programming, the main purpose of a *package* is to organize the related assets of a program. This includes classes and *interfaces*. Keep in mind that packages are literally just the *namespace, identifier,* or just *name* given to the location where these assets are organized. Think of packages as the individual folders you create and name in your computer.

Creating the Main Class

Upon creating your first project, a *main class* as well as the package containing it should be created automatically by default. If not, you can manually create this class by clicking *File* → *New File* from the main menu (NetBeans shortcut: *Ctrl + N*). Create a new *Java Class.*

The main class plays a key role in any Java application. It contains the *main method,* which is executed first in a program written in Java. This is called the *entry point* in a program and is present in other programming languages as well.

The 'Hello World' Application

The *Hello World* application is an iconic application used in many programming languages. This simple program will display the message *"Hello World"* on your computer screen. It is created with only one purpose: to allow students to understand the basic program structure of their chosen language and to give you the quickest possible orientation with the Java program structure, you will be introduced to the simplest possible application in the world of programming:

```
1
2    package myfirstproject;
3
4    public class MyFirstProject {
5
6        public static void main(String[] args) {
7
8            System.out.println("Hello World!");
9        }
10
11    }
12
13
```

The Hello World Application

There are *three essential program parts* in the Hello World application. These are the *package statement, class declaration,* and the *methods.* In line 2, you can find the **package statement** which is represented by the syntax:

package myfirstproject;

This statement is *optional* if the code is written solely for testing purposes. In which case, Java will consider the program to belong in the *default package.* The default package is merely an untitled package. However, if you are working on a project, it is important that the package statement reflects the namespace of the package that contains the class. For now, make sure that the identifier matches the package wherein you created the class. For most IDEs, the package is automatically created along with a main class that is used as reference to it.

Next in line 4 is the **class declaration** for the class "MyFirstProject". It is written in the syntax:

public class MyFirstProject

The open curly brace "{" denotes the beginning of the class. Always remember that each open curly brace should have a closing brace "}" to tell the program where a specific code block ends. In the Hello World program, notice that the MyFirstProject class ended *after* the rest of the code sections was executed.

Notice the word public in this class declaration. This is an example of an *access modifier,* which implements *encapsulation* or the control of other classes from accessing certain information. Public simply means the information can be accessed by all other classes. If it is set to *private,* then only the current class can access it. In something as simple as the Hello World program, you can forget access modifiers and the program will still run correctly.

Coding Convention: Making the Main Class Public

Coding conventions are set guidelines or standards considered as the recommended practices for coding. You will learn more about the essential coding conventions as you go through this book. The first convention you need to adopt is the setting of the main class as a public class.

Lastly in line 6 is the beginning of the **main method**, which is defined in the syntax:

public static void main(String[] args)

Aside from the public modifier, there are two other keywords present in the main method declaration: *static* and *void*. The static keyword means that the attached field is related to the class and not the instances and objects under it. This allows the program to access it freely and run the method without having to create an instance under that class. This is crucial for the main method since it is the entry point of the program.

Next is the *void* return type. This allows the program to inform the *JVM* or *Java virtual machine* that it ran and finished correctly. Lastly, the parameters inside the parentheses "String[] args" are necessary to support *command-line arguments.*

Coding Convention: Using 'args'

Bear in mind that you can replace args with anything you like. However, it is an established coding convention to use args specifically for the main method.

The blocks of code inside the Hello World program represent the most basic sections in a Java program, but what about the statements inside the main method that tell the program exactly what to do? What exactly is the method used to make the program print the words; *Hello World*? If the classes, objects, and instances are the sectors of a program, then the *statements* that fall within these sections of code are the building blocks. These will be discussed in the next chapter.

CHAPTER 3

How to Get User Input

The very essence of programming is to establish communication between man and machine. In the Java programming language, there are *Input/Output* or *I/O streams* that enable communication between the program and the end user. You have already utilized the output stream on the previous chapter by printing information. This time, you will learn how to improve this communication and allow the end user to create *inputs.*

Chapter Overview:

**The Basic Output Syntax for Java*

**Getting User Input*

**Printing out User Input*

Before proceeding with getting user input, let us review how you utilized the output stream in the Hello World program. Inside the main method in line 8, you can find the syntax:

System.out.println("Hello World!");

Note that a **capital 'S'** must be used since Java is a case-sensitive programming language. This is the basic syntax that feeds whatever is inside the parentheses and double quotation marks into the output stream of the Java program. Take note that there is actually another way to do this. You can use the syntax:

System.out.print("Hello World!");

The main difference is that the command println is replaced with just *print*. The difference between the two is that println will print the information on a *new line.*

Using this simple statement, you can easily modify what the Hello World program will print out. You can make it print something like "Hi there, cousin" or "Congratulations on your first program". So far, you have managed to create a program that allows a *one-way communication* (program → user). Next, you will learn how to allow the end user to communicate back to the program using *user input* (user → program → user).

Getting User Input

In Java, you can take advantage of a built-in class called a *Scanner* to quickly and easily get user input. The purpose of the Scanner is that it gets information from the input stream, usually from the *keyboard,* and stores it into a *variable.*

Before you can use the scanner, you need to add the following line in your program:

import java.util.Scanner;

What you see is an *import statement,* which basically imports a class from a local package. In this specific usage, you are importing the

Scanner class from the java.util package. To actually use or *call* the Scanner class in a program, you will have to use the following statement:

Scanner VariableName = new Scanner(System.in);

In this example, the class Scanner which was imported was called to initialize a variable called 'VariableName'. Take note that you can change this name to whatever you prefer. Next comes the *assignment operator* (=) followed by the statement new Scanner(System.in);. Basically, this tells the program that the value of VariableName must be assigned based on the user input.

Coding Convention: Variable Naming

It is an established coding convention to capitalize the first letter of the words in a variable name. For example, instead of declaring a variable as 'johndoe', you should declare it instead as 'JohnDoe'.

The quickest way to utilize user input is to use the output stream to show what the user has typed into the program. Using the standard output statement, you can use the following syntax to print out the user input:

System.out.println(VariableName.nextLine());

The nextLine() method will tell the program to *return a string value* that was inserted into the current line. Note that you can also scan other data types like *numbers* with the Scanner class. This will be discussed in the next chapter. Using this method will also basically tell the program to wait until it finishes searching for input, so the program will not advance until the user types something and presses enter.

Furthermore, remember that you can also use this output statement with textual information to be printed out along the Scanner variable. All you have to do is to use the *additive operator* (+) inside the parentheses. For example, you can use the following syntax:

System.out.println("You typed " +VariableName.nextLine());

Say the user inserted "Bananas". Instead of printing just "Bananas", the program will now print out "You typed Bananas".

Take a look at this program and notice how it uses the Scanner class to get user input:

```
1
2    package myfirstproject;
3  ⊟ import java.util.Scanner;
4
5    class MyFirstProject {
6
7  ⊟    public static void main(String[] args) {
8
9            System.out.println("What is your name?");
10           Scanner VariableName = new Scanner(System.in);
11           System.out.println("Hey there, " +VariableName.nextLine());
12
13
14       }
15
16   }
```

In this scenario, the words "What is your name?" is displayed to prompt the user to insert his name. After which, the program prints out user input with the words "Hey there, ". Congratulations, you have now achieved a two-way communication in a Java program!

Moving on...

As mentioned above, the Scanner class will store information into a variable. Keep in mind that a Scanner variable will not work like other variables, but what exactly are variables in the first place?

CHAPTER 4

How to Declare and Use Variables

An application that does not utilize or operate with data is hardly an application at all. For example, the Hello World will always have the same output no matter how many times you try to run it. This is why the next lesson is all about using *variables,* which will allow you to create data with different and non-constant values.

Chapter Overview:

**How to Declare and Use Variables

**All about Data Types

**Using Other Data Types with the Input Stream

Variables are used in programming languages as *containers* for pieces of data. Logical and arithmetic operations can be performed using the values of variables. These operations control the logic of an application. Variables need to be declared before you can use them in the program. Lastly, a data type should be specified upon declaration of a variable. It can be an integer, a character, a Boolean value, or other numbers with different bit sizes; namely *float, double, long, short,* and *byte.*

Here is a brief explanation on each data type:

- **Integer** – The simplest data type for handling numbers that can be used in the Java programming language is the integer. When an **int** variable is declared without a value, it will automatically be assigned to 0. An int variable may not contain decimal points, so it is not ideal for precision data.

- **String** – The **string** data type is for containing a sequence of alphanumeric characters. A string declared without an assigned value will automatically be given a *null* value.

- **Character** – The **char** variable accepts a single character as data. By default, the value of a char variable will be *\u0000,* which represents an empty space.

- **Boolean** – The **Boolean** data type may have two different values; *true* or *false.* By default, a Boolean variable will automatically be initialized as false.

- **Short** – The difference between int and the other numerical data types could be the presence of decimal points *or* the range of numbers allowed. The **short** data type may contain a *16-bit signed 2s integer* (from *-32,768* to *32,767*). The default value of a short variable is 0.

- **Long** – The **long** data type may contain a *64-bit signed 2s complement integer (-9,223,372,036,854,775,808* to *9,223,372,036,854,775,807).* The default value of a long variable is 0.

- **Byte** – In all the number data types, the **byte** has the smallest range. It may contain an *8-bit signed 2s complement integer.* The default value of a byte variable is 0.

- **Float** – The **float** data type is used for *32-bit IEEE 754* numerical values. These numbers basically have decimal points. The default value for a float variable is 0.0f.

- **Double** – The **double** data type may contain a *64-bit IEEE 754,* which is more precise than float. The default value for a double variable is 0.0d.

Declaring Variables

When declaring variables, a namespace or identifier is assigned with a data type. For example, you can use the following syntax to declare a variable called 'MyVar' with the *integer* data type:

int MyVar = 0;

Take note that the default value will be assigned if this integer is declared with the following syntax:

int MyVar;

Variables with other data types can be declared in the same way. All you have to do is to declare the data type first and then decide an identifier for the variable. Also, make sure that an assigned value is appropriate for the data type should you choose to specify it upon declaration. Let us declare the variable MyVar using all the data types with their default values:

Note: Remember that Java is case-sensitive. This includes the syntax for declaring variables.

- **Boolean** – Boolean MyVar; **or** Boolean MyVar = false;

- **String** – String MyVar; **or** String MyVar = null;

- **Character** – char MyVar;

- **Short** – short MyVar; **or** short MyVar = 0;

- **Long** – long MyVar; **or** long MyVar = 0L;

- **Byte** – byte Myvar; **or** byte MyVar = 0;

- **Float** – float MyVar; **or** float MyVar = 0.0f;

- **Double** – double MyVar; **or** double MyVar = 0.0d;

Getting Other Data

In the previous chapter, a Scanner variable was declared when the Scanner class was used. The specific example in the previous chapter accepted a *string* value. However, you can also use the Scanner class to collect other types of data from the input stream. Let's say you want the user to input an integer that will represent his or her age. Instead of using nextLine(), you will be using *nextInt()* to tell the program to save an *integer* data type. Take a look at the program below:

```
1
2    package myfirstproject;
3  ⊟ import java.util.Scanner;
4
5    class MyFirstProject {
6
7  ⊟    public static void main(String[] args) {
8
9          System.out.println("What is your age?");
10         Scanner VariableName = new Scanner(System.in);
11         System.out.println("Your age is " +VariableName.nextInt());
12
13
14      }
15
16   }
17
```

This program will show an integer data type that the user has typed. Observe that nextInt() was used next to the Scanner variable. You may also use a Scanner variable with the integer data type for simple arithmetic operations. For example, take a look at the program below:

```
1
2    package myfirstproject;
3  ⊟ import java.util.Scanner;
4
5    class MyFirstProject {
6
7  ⊟    public static void main(String[] args) {
8
9          System.out.println("What is your age?");
10         Scanner VariableName = new Scanner(System.in);
11         System.out.println("Ten years from now, you will be " +(VariableName.nextInt()+10));
12
13
14      }
15
16   }
17
```

Notice the following syntax in line 11:

System.out.println("Ten years from now, you will be "
+(VariableName.nextInt()+10));

Keep in mind that arithmetic operations printed this way should be enclosed in parentheses in order for them to be processed properly. For example, if the user inputs *2*, then the resulting number will be 12. However, the resulting number will be *210* (2+10) if the following syntax is used:

> System.out.println("Ten years from now, you will be
> "+VariableName.NextInt+10);

Aside from integers, you can scan for other data types:

1. **Byte** – nextByte()

2. **Short** – nextShort()

3. **Long** – nextLong()

4. **Float** – nextFloat()

5. **Double** – nextDouble()

Saving Input into Variables

To save user input into a useable variable, you need to declare the variable you want to use first. This will allow you to create more elaborate operations in your program, especially if you will be using multiple values from user input. Remember that you should already have an idea in mind on what the data type of that variable should be. For example, take a look at the program below:

```
    package myfirstproject;
 □  import java.util.Scanner;

    class MyFirstProject {

 □      public static void main(String[] args) {

            int MyVar = 0;
            System.out.println("Insert a number");
            Scanner VariableName = new Scanner(System.in);
            MyVar = VariableName.nextInt();
            System.out.println("The final value is " +MyVar);

        }

    }
```

Notice that instead of printing the Scanner variable VariableName directly, it was first saved into MyVar. This integer variable was then used to print the user input from the scanner class.

CHAPTER 5

How to Use Operators

In Java, many operators are used to control, modify, and compare data. One operator you have been using for a while now is the assignment operator which is represented by the equal sign (=). The assignment operator works by saving a compatible value into a variable. However, it doesn't necessarily have to be a set value. You can use arithmetic operators to control the value that will be assigned to a variable.

Chapter Overview:

**Performing Basic Mathematical Computations*

**Performing Logical Operations*

**Performing Bit Wise Operations*

Simply put, performing mathematical computations in a computer program requires the use of similar operators taught in school, and the fastest way to learn about arithmetic operations in Java is to see them in action. Now that you know how to save user input into a separate variable, let us try constructing a simple program that *adds* two numbers from user input. Take a look at the program below:

```
package myfirstproject;
import java.util.Scanner;

class MyFirstProject {

    public static void main(String[] args) {

        int Number1, Number2, Sum;
        System.out.println("Insert the first number");
        Scanner VariableName = new Scanner(System.in);
        Number1 = VariableName.nextInt();
        System.out.println("Insert the second number");
        Number2 = VariableName.nextInt();
        Sum = Number1 + Number2;
        System.out.println("The sum of the two numbers is " +Sum);

    }

}
```

In this particular example, 3 integer variables were used: **Number1, Number2,** and **Sum.** Notice how they were all initialized in the same line with their default values. You can do the same thing with other data types when declaring multiple variables. If you want to set a value for a specific variable when declaring them this way, you can use the syntax:

int Number1 = 1, Number2 = 2, Sum = 0;

Basically, the variables Number1 and Number2 will be used to contain the two numbers from user input. A separate variable named Sum is then created to contain the sum of the two numbers. You can see the addition being done in the syntax:

Sum = Number1 + Number2;

Understanding and knowing how to use operators is an essential step in programming with Java. All you have to learn is what the symbol for each operator is and you can easily implement them into your program. Without further ado, here is the list of the essential operators in Java:

Arithmetic

The most basic form of operators aside from the assignment operator is the arithmetic operators. These are the following:

- **+ *Additive Operator*** – Returns the sum of two values.

- **- *Subtractive Operator*** – Returns the difference of two values.

- *** *Multiplicative Operator*** – Returns the product of two values.

- **/ *Divisive Operator*** – Returns the quotient of two values.

- **% *Remainder Operator*** – Divides two numbers and returns the remainder.

Increment/Decrement Operators

Next are the *increment* and *decrement* operators that increase and decrease a value by 1, respectively.

- *++ Increment*

- *-- Decrement*

Keep in mind that these can be used either as a *prefix* or *postfix*. If used as a prefix, the value will be adjusted immediately when it is used. However, as a postfix, the value will be returned first before it is adjusted. For example, if MyVar = 3:

- *MyVar++ ; The returned value is still 3*

- *++MyVar ; The returned value will be adjusted to 4*

Theoretically, both will increase the value of MyVar by 1. It's just that the postfix increment operator will update this value *after* returning the original value.

Logic Operators

There are also other operators you can use to compare two values or set specific conditions. The significance of these operators is they permit a degree of *flow control* to your program. You can use these operators to set different outcomes for your program. Depending on the two values to be compared, a Boolean value can be returned which may also be used to determine whether a certain block of code will be run or not. This is the basest form of logic in a computer program.

These operators comprise of the *relational* or *equality operators* and *conditional operators*. If what they are checking is true, they will return the Boolean value 'true':

- == **Is Equal to** – This will check if two values are equal.

- != **Is Not Equal to** – This will check if two values are unequal.

- > **Is Greater than** – This checks if the operand to the left is greater than the operand to the right.

- < **Is Less than** – This checks if the operand to the left is less than the operand to the right.

- >= **Is Greater than or Equal** – This checks if the operand to the left is greater than or equal to the operand to the right.

- <= **Is Less than or Equal** – This checks if the operand to the left is less than or equal to the operand on the right.

- && **Logical AND** – This checks if both operands are true.

- || **Logical OR** – This checks if at least one of the operands area true.

The best way to use these operators is to create flow control statements that will open up a whole new world of possibilities in your Java programming capabilities. Feel free to return to this chapter if you need reference. Once you're ready, let us try to create a simple *game* with what you've learned with Java so far.

Bit Wise Operators

There are operators that take into account the variables in a program and have them manipulated, at the bit level; these operators are called *bit wise operators*. In processes where binary numerals are required, they are called to provide value or be used for comparison.

Moreover, bit wise operators are known to be both primitive and fast. They hasten processes due to their need for a reduced source (i.e. binary numerals are the sources). Since binary numerals are defined as the smallest units of addressable memory, they can analyze the usual processes in a dash.

Bit wise operators:

- **And (or &)** – This is a 2 equal-length binary operator; it performs with the employment of the logic operator *AND* and multiplies both of the elements with bits.

- **Not (or ~)** – This is a unary operator; it performs with the goal of logical negation; its purpose is to complement the binary value of ones

- **Or (or |)** – This is an operator that takes 2-bit patterns whose lengths are equal; it performs with the employment of the logic operator *OR* and expects results that are usually 0 or 1.

- **Xor (or ^)** – This is an operator that, like the *Or bit wise operator*, takes 2-bit patterns whose lengths are equal; unlike the Or bit wise operator, however, the results are expected to defined with a similar digit.

CHAPTER 6

How to Use Flow Control

As a future Java programmer, you will want an interactive experience without being too predictable. This chapter is a straightforward answer that will allow you to create an easy and simple program that can have countless possibilities. After all, this is the best way to be introduced to the *flow control statements* and Java's built-in random number generator.

Chapter Overview:

**Generating Random Numbers

**Using Flow Control Statements

To generate a random number, we will need to import the *Random* class from the java.util package. The correct syntax for this is:

import java.util.Random;

Calling the Random class in your program is quite similar when using the Scanner class. Just like the Scanner class, a Random variable will also be declared. Here is the syntax for generating a random number:

Random VariableName = new Random();

Just like when using the Scanner class, you can save the random number you got from the Random class into a new variable:

```
import java.util.Random;

class MyFirstProject {

    public static void main(String[] args)
    {
        int MyRandomNumber;
        Random VariableName = new Random();
        MyRandomNumber = VariableName.nextInt();
        System.out.println(MyRandomNumber);

    }
```

Flow Control Statements

By now, you should have noticed that a class programmed with Java runs in *one direction* - from the topmost line to the bottom. However, you can use *logical statements* and *looping statements* to modify the flow of your program. Here is an introduction to these statements and how to use them.

If-Then-Else

The **if-then-else** statement is the most basic flow control statement. In the previous chapter, you learned about *logical operators,* which can be used to determine whether or not a specific condition is fulfilled. For the correct syntax for an if-then-else statement, take a look at the codes below:

```
class MyFirstProject {

    public static void main(String[] args)
    {
    int InQuestion;
    System.out.println("Insert the number 5.");
    Scanner ScannedNumber = new Scanner(System.in);
    InQuestion = ScannedNumber.nextInt();
    if (InQuestion == 5)
    {
        System.out.println("Thank you!");
    } else
    {
        System.out.println("Please follow the instructions.");
    }

}
}
```

Here, the condition to be tested is **if** the variable **InQuestion** is equal to 5 (refer to logic operators in the previous chapter). Also, notice that the value of the variable InQuestion is obtained from the user input. If the user inputs the number 5, then the methods inside the *if* block will be executed ("Thank you!").

However, if the condition is not met, the **else** block will be run instead ("Please follow the instructions") while the methods inside the if block will be ignored completely. Bear in mind that an else block is optional. Without it, the program will just proceed to the rest of the class in case the condition isn't met.

Loops

A looping statement in programming allows methods to be run and rerun as long as specific conditions are met. There are three types of loops in Java; the *while loop, do-while loop,* and *for loop.* To demonstrate the syntax for these loops, they will be used to create a simple countdown from 10 to 1.

- **While loop** – The *while loop* will rerun the methods inside the block while the specified condition is met. Depending on the condition, a while loop may *never* run even once.

```
int InQuestion = 10;
while (InQuestion > 0)
{
    System.out.println(InQuestion);
    InQuestion--;
}
```

- **Do-while loop** – The main difference between a while loop and a do-while loop is that the methods inside a do-while loop is sure to run at least *once* before the condition is checked.

```
int InQuestion = 10;
do
{
    System.out.println(InQuestion);
    InQuestion--;
} while (InQuestion > 0);
```

- **For loop** – Lastly, a for loop is declared with specific *parameters* that control the life cycle of the loop. Variables that can be used to control the for loop may be declared simultaneously with the loop itself.

```
for(int InQuestion = 10; InQuestion > 0; InQuestion--)
{
    System.out.println(InQuestion);
}
```

The Dice Game

To wrap up everything you have learned about Java so far, here is a simple *dice-rolling game* that makes use of user input, variables, mathematical operations, as well as a random number generator and looping statements:

```
8   public static void main(String[] args)
9   {
10      String Try;
11      int Dice1;
12      int Dice2;
13      int Total;
14
15      System.out.println("Press R to roll! 12 to win!");
16      Scanner AnyKey = new Scanner(System.in);
17      Try = AnyKey.next();
18      while (Try.equals("R") || Try.equals("r"))
19      {
20          Random RandomNumber = new Random();
21          Dice1 = RandomNumber.nextInt((6 - 1) +1) + 1;
22          System.out.println("The first die rolls " + Dice1);
23          Dice2 = RandomNumber.nextInt((6 - 1) +1) + 1;
24          System.out.println("The second die rolls " + Dice2);
25          Total = Dice1 + Dice2;
26          System.out.println("You rolled " + Total);
27          if (Total == 12)
28          {
29              System.out.println("You win!");
30          }
31          else
32          {
33              System.out.println("You lose!");
34          }
35          System.out.println("Press R to roll again!");
36          Scanner Retry = new Scanner(System.in);
37          Try = Retry.nextLine();
38      }
39  }
40  }
```

Program Guide:

- **From line 10-13** – The variables for the core program are declared.

- **Line 15** – The user is prompted to press R to play the game.

- **From line 16-17** – The user input is saved into the variable 'Try'.

- **Line 18** – A while loop is initialized.

- **From line 20-24** – The Random class is used to generate random numbers, which are saved into variables **Dice1** and **Dice2**. In this example, the possible outcomes are restricted to values from 1 to 6 only to reflect the sides of the dice. The formula for setting minimum and maximum values in random number generators is: nextInt((max – min) + min) +min;

- **Line 25** – The values of **Dice1** and **Dice2** are added and saved into the variable **Total**.

- **Line 26** – The value of **Total** is printed.

- **Line 27** – An **if-then** statement is used to congratulate the user if **Total** equals 12.

- **Line 31** – If **Total** is not equal to 12, an **else** statement is used.

- **Line 35** – The user is asked if he or she wishes to try again.

- **From line 36-37** – The Scanner class is used again to redefine the value of '**Try**'.

CHAPTER 7

How to Use Access Modifiers

In the previous chapters, you were introduced to the basic classes, fields, and methods in Java; when using them, as well as declaring different statements in the programming language, *access modifiers* enter the picture. This chapter is about the particular modifiers, or the ones that *categorize the components* of an entire design for the flawless processes during eventual execution.

Alongside, access modifiers are useful for *encapsulation* or data hiding. Other than helping you structure your program accordingly, they are responsible for regulating the accessibility levels of previously declared commands and functions. They make sure your written language remains clean; if the access of just any variable is restricted, it is due to the instruction of an access modifier.

Let's put it like this: by introducing a specific method in your program, you grant access to other methods using an access modifier as basis. If the access modifier in subject is rather protective, and it doesn't allow access from an unlisted method, your program stays safe the execution of that method.

Chapter Overview

Learning about the Various Types of Access Modifiers

Comparing Various Types of Access Modifiers

**Using Access Modifiers*

Types of Access Modifiers

Access modifiers come in types so they can be used for the proper imposition of accessibility levels. For one, they make it easy for a programmer to analyze his own program; a beginner, especially, will appreciate the fact that the different modifiers are not generalized as one. For another, they make it less challenging for a fellow programmer to pick up on a previous programmer's progress; instead of having to start from scratch or rack his brains out as he attempts to understand pre-determined commands and functions, as well as previously declared statements, he can simply rely on a certain access levels.

Java access modifiers:

- **Default** – This is the type of modifier that comes to the rescue when a programmer did not specify an access modifier. Due to the absence of a particular keyword, any command or function can access a portion of a program; however, its availability is limited to access by fields that belong to a similar package. Without a modifier, a program can be effective yet be quite unclean. Also, since no keyword was noted, the level of access is usually open to the public; a program may be available publicly, but it isn't included in an interface. Sample:

```
String version = "1.88.1"

Boolean process_order () {

       return true

}
```

In the sample above, a string order version in a program was declared. Since a specific type of access modifier is undefined, any command or function can be used to access the program component; thus, its Boolean logic, *process_order*, can be modified easily.

- **Private** – This type of modifier is known to accommodate the most restrictive fields in a program; it cannot be accessed, and therefore, employed with just any command or function. It encourages the observance of strict protocols; if a particular instruction is from an unlisted source, or is quite vague, it cannot be granted recognition.

In the case when a new programmer steps in to continue the work of a previous programmer, his job becomes a notch challenging; if certain program components are specified with private access modifiers, he should be careful when introducing new commands and functions since these may be unidentifiable. His options include the re-declaration of past statements and regulating ALL access modifiers. Sample:

```
public class arcadia extends bay {

    private int name_of_residents
    private boolean in_city

    public arcadia () {
        name_of_residents = joy
        in_city = false
    }
    private void shrill ()
    system.out.printIn (quiet);

    public void action ()
    system.out.printIn (talk);


    }

}
```

In the sample above, the public class *arcadia* is defined; it is, then, allowed an extensive function, *bay*. Although arcadia bay is accessible publicly, some of its internal properties (e.g. name_of_residents and shrill), as well as its Boolean logic, in_city, are set to private. In such a case, since one of its internal components, *action*, is set to public, it can, therefore, be acknowledged by different fields.

- **Public** – This is the type of access modifier that allows access from just about any other field. With a public access level, it's less laborious for a programmer to visit other parts of his work. Thus, all the commands and functions, as well as the different components of a program, which belong to a public class can be accessed via a recognized instruction in Java programming language.

  However, a public access modifier comes with its own batch of limitations, too. Despite the fact that all commands and functions are set to public (and thus, are categorized under the other elements in the Java universe), it cannot be accessed by classes that belong to a different package. In the event when a programmer intends to access a particular restriction, the solution is to set another modifier, or have the restrictions imported.

  Public access modifiers are used often; they typically start with:

```
public static void  (string arguments) {

    // ..

    }
```

- **Protected** – This is a type of access modifier that belongs to a *superclass*. It means 2 things: (1) it can only be accessed by the fields that are declared in a particular superclass, and (2) it can only be accessed by the subclasses of a similar package. The goal of the categorization is to improve program structure while restricting the access of an irrelevant element.

  Moreover, the protected type of access modifier imposes strict protocols. Its application is rather limited; particularly, it cannot be applied to classes and interfaces. Any field can be declared as protected, but only if it is not affiliated to any class or interface. Sample:

```
class seven_fields

    protected boolean open_fields (field1 sp) {

        // implementation

    }

}

class opening seven_fields (field1 sp) {

    // implementation

    }

}
```

In the sample above, the class, *seven_fields*, was declared. Since it is under the protected access modifier, its Boolean logic, *open_fields* (i.e. an instruction for the opening of field 1) is inaccessible with the use of just any command or function. Unless he declares a new access modifier, a programmer cannot have the particular part of the program modified.

Comparing Access Modifiers

Of the 4 access modifiers, many programmers propose that relying on default accessibility is best; this is suggested especially for a beginner in Java, who could benefit from the opportunity to access different fields with the use of just about any command or function. The particular preference grants him the freedom to return to a previous program component without the need to modify a structure.

Private, and public access modifiers, on the other hand, are capable of causing too significant an impact on a program. Private accessibility is too restrictive and too closed; public accessibility is too open and can often confuse another programmer.

Meanwhile, the impact of a protected access modifier is similar to that of default accessibility; this rewards versatility to a programmer, regarding possible program revisions. In a way, it is both available to a private crowd and to a public crowd, but only to *specific* authorities.

Thus, the main decision regarding the correct access modifier for a program depends on the goal. Determine what you're trying to achieve, as well as who a program is for. It may not be recommended, but if a program is intended for a public crowd, setting the accessibility level to public is the more practical option.

Systematic Approach

The use of access modifiers is almost effortless with the goal of encapsulation. Once you have decided on a particular type of keyword, the job can be accomplished easily. However, since Java programming, like most programming languages, can be quite stern regarding declarations, it's a must to practice caution with every new introduction. Otherwise, a feature of a program, or worse, an entire program, may not work accordingly.

3 steps:

1. **Choose the appropriate access modifier.** Determine whether the best one to use is *default, private, public,* or *protected.*

2. **Declare the access modifier.** Key in the word *default, private, public,* or *protected.*

   Sample # 1 (default access modifier):

   default static string default ()

   {

          return "This is default accessibility."

   }

   Sample # 2 (protected access modifier):

   protected static string protected ()

   {

          return "This is protected accessibility."

   }

3. **Check the program.** This is a very important step. Screen a program for incorrect declarations and misspelled words. Before proceeding to the next portion, always make sure that this part is fully accomplished.

CHAPTER 8

How to Use Classes & Objects

Since it is an object-oriented language, among the best features of Java is its support for both *classes* and objects. With the feature, a Java program can accommodate advanced commands and functions. And, just like the others, it allows a program to accomplish logical tasks. Alongside, it defines an operation that can retain its use all throughout program execution.

Chapter Overview

**Understanding Classes

**Understanding Objects

**Distinguishing the Difference between Classes & Objects

**Learning the Basics of Encapsulation

**Learning about the Abstraction Process

**Understanding the Purpose of Attributes

What are Classes?

Classes are templates or blueprints that are in charge of describing the characteristics of an element. They can have any number of elements or methods to accommodate the accessibility levels of other methods.

Moreover, classes are behind the reason why a programmer who merely picked up on the progress of a previous programmer can understand a program. Since the templates define elements, it is less challenging for a new fellow to decode a former signature. Especially if the programmer in subject is a beginner, program structure becomes clear.

List of possible class variables:

- **Instance** – This is a variable outside of a method, but remains within a particular class. When that class is instantiated, it requires initial declaration. Once declared, it is accessible from any other method in a program.

- **Local** – This is a variable that is defined inside any method in the program. Within that method, it requires initial declaration, as well as acknowledgement until its inclusion becomes unnecessary. After it has completed its command or function, it should be omitted.

- **Class** – This is a variable that needs to be declared before it enters a class. It can be found inside any class and outside any method.

What Are Objects?

Objects are elements that come with behaviors and states. Once defined, elements can come with their own features; this grants them the chance to add value to a program component without requiring an extensive structure. As it follows, they are instances of classes.

Methods can be executed successfully due to the behaviors and states of objects. For the accomplishment of a task, a particular object is associated with a unique command or function. This way, they can adhere to certain instructions.

Moreover, you will be introduced to 3 relationships of an object. These relationships become apparent as you turn to the elements every time; they hold the explanation as to why the elements *should and should not* be moved to a particular program component.

The 3 object relationships:

1. **Is-a relationship** – This object relationship means that a type of object is more specific than its fellows. For example, number 1; *number 1 is a number*.

2. **Has-a relationship** – This object relationship means that a type of object contains or is associated with another object. For example, the relationship between number 1 and number 2; *number 2 has a succeeding number, number 2*.

3. **Uses-a relationship** – This object relationship means that a type of object will be using another object as a program progresses. For example, the relationship between number 1, number 2, and number 3; *number 1 uses a number 2 to arrive at the sum of number 3*.

Classes vs. Objects

Classes and objects are often mentioned together; thus, there are a few who confuse them as one and the same. In many cases, a programmer who can easily distinguish the difference between the 2 elements exhibit technical aptness. Especially if at a beginner's level, a programmer can identify the unique qualities of each element, that individual may be looking at a great career in Java programming.

A factor that needs consideration when comparing classes and objects is that *classes do not have a lifespan*; however, *objects are known to have a lifespan*. This means that while the former can remain in a program as long as desired, or when a programmer writes an instruction to have it omitted, the latter operates with a deadline, and is usually omitted once a process is complete.

A common concern regarding the lifespan of objects is their effect on classes. Addressed to experts in Java programming are different versions of the question: *"If they are written out of a program, will the classes they belong in remain valid?"* In such a case, only the objects of that class have lost their validity, and *not the entire class*.

Thus, classes are generic elements in Java programming. Objects, on the other hand, contain specific descriptions of an element, and their presence in a program is rather limited. If they are no longer needed to perform a specific function, they are forgotten.

Encapsulation 101

In the previous chapter, *encapsulation* was briefly defined as *data-hiding*; in a chapter that focuses on classes and objects, granting a better perspective of encapsulation to a programmer is practical. This is due to the elements that he will be encapsulating; they are classes and objects.

Encapsulation is actually a fundamental concept in the programming universe in general. In the data-hiding process, classes and objects are not hidden randomly nor are random classes and objects hidden; instead, the elements are thoroughly evaluated. It is only the elements that may not affect a program's performance that are hidden. Each one undergoes a screening process, and through this screening process, its value is determined.

The Abstraction Process

Abstraction is a process that revolves around 2 concepts: (1) the identification of both classes and objects and (2) the categorization of both classes and objects into types. As it identifies and categorizes, it screens an element thoroughly and decides which group to sort them in. In this stage, a program will observe that although there are similarities regarding the behaviors and states of particular elements, they are actually very different.

As it follows, an important step of creating a Java program is the abstraction process or the creation of abstract categories. This allows a programmer to group certain elements and filter them according to their defining behaviors and states.

Where Do Attributes Fit in?

After identifying classes and objects, a programmer's job is, then, required to focus on the more definitive nature of the elements; the definitive nature, in subject, are referred to as *attributes*. They emphasize the fact that different elements carry their own integral feature in a program. Therefore, the nature of particular elements is described by their attributes. Sample:

```
public class number_1 {

    number_1 ();

    system.out.println (number_1 is a number);

    system.out.println (number_1 comes before number_2);

    }

}
```

In the sample above, it is shown that the 2 attributes of the element *number_1* are: (1) number 1 is a number and (2) number_1 comes before number_2.

CHAPTER 9

How to Use Constructors

Previously, you learned about classes and objects. In this chapter, you're going to understand the importance of knowing that there are various methods that allows the declaration of such elements. Alongside, you'll also be given a lesson on the need to avoid the generalization of all components in the Java programming universe.

One of such methods is the use of *constructors*; they are methods that work as superb commands. Unlike the ordinary instructions, their execution can be behind the most interesting aspects of the programming language.

Chapter Overview

***Learning about the Purpose of Constructors**

***Understanding Constructors**

***Understanding the Difference between Constructors & Methods**

***Knowing that Constructor Overload Is Possible**

What Are Constructors?

Constructors are methods that serve as parameters of different types. As the rules of Java dictate, every time they are invoked, they need to match the other elements in a pre-defined function. It was created similarly to others in its category; it is not known to return a value.

While a constructor can be defined, Java is one of the programming languages that can provide a default constructor. This default constructor, however, is not designed to carry out tasks; although it can set parameters, it cannot perform unique actions and cannot take any argument. Thus, an explicit version is necessary for the approval of particular commands and functions.

The main purpose of constructors is to initialize the call to a fellow constructor by declaring *special ()*. Upon the acknowledgement of a new constructor, a programmer is encouraged to create and set a parameter for the introduction of an object.

"This" & "Super"

Constructors are known to be affiliated with the keyword *this*. Just like the typical Java programming methods, the keyword is used to pertain to a particular program component. And, in most cases, the keyword is employed as reference to other constructors in a similar class, but in different parameter list. Sample:

```
public class dolphin {
    string name;
    dolphin (string input) {
    }
    dolphin () {
        this ("hazel / michelle");
    }
    public static void int main (string arguments []) {
    dolphin p1 = new dolphin ("john")
    dolphin p2 = new dolphin ();
    }
}
```

In the sample above, the constructor use of *this* refers to other constructors named *hazel* and *michelle* under the public class *dolphin*. The strings have defined arguments and 2 batches of parameters (e.g. john for p1 and default constructor for p2) are set.

On the other hand, constructors are also known to use *super*; usually, it can be identified in the 1st line since program compilers that run a Java don't return a value if *super* is not declared initially. Unlike other methods, the employment of the keyword is accomplished to invoke a superclass constructor. Sample:

```
public class super superclass_penta {
    super superclass_penta () {}
}
class tonics extends superclass_penta
    tonics () {
        super ();
    }
}
```

In the sample above, the constructor use of *super* defines the superclass_penta; it is categorized under the class *tonics*. Although a class is already known to be previously defined, the capability of a special constructor performance is possible.

Constructor vs. Any Method

By its very definition, constructors are also methods; this is why constructors and methods are often confused to be one and the same. However, they are not since the latter is a generic version of the former.

A notable aspect that emphasizes the difference between constructor and generic methods? Each element differs when it comes to return types. While constructors aren't known to have any return type (i.e. it doesn't incorporate void when returning a value), methods finish a program component with valid return keywords of sorts.

Moreover, constructors and generic methods differ in terms of each of their signatures. On one hand, constructors are observed to carry the names of their class; usually, they begin with an uppercase letter. Methods, on the other hand, are never associated with names of their class and are noticed to start with a lowercase letter.

Turning to the Compiler Code

In some cases when using constructors, a Java programmer may encounter compilers that will be the ones to supply the codes for a program's constructors. This is a result of the failure to specify a constructor during the beginning, especially when the compiler sees fit that a particular keyword should be defined.

An automatically supplied code can be recognized normally in the form of:

```
public class This_is_a_constructor {}
```

Constructors Overload

Since they are capable of getting overloaded, constructors can be defined numerously and still perform instructions effectively. Just make sure an initial value (i.e. a value that will serve as the core constructor) is declared, so a program can adhere to the main instruction. The result of this is to accomplish a series of commands and functions without the hassle of complicated and misleading statements; this is especially useful for a programmer, even if he is still a novice in Java. Sample:

```
public class c_delta (string first, string second, string last)

{

        first = alpha;

        second = gamma;

        last - omega;

}
```

In the sample above, the class *c_delta* comes with a series of constructors: the first named *alpha,* the second named *gamma*, and the last named o*mega*. It eliminates possible confusion for a programmer since initial values were defined.

CHAPTER 10

How Serials Affect a Program

Back in the 1960s, one of the first technological advancements in the world of computing is *serial communication*. It served as a n effective of transferring important information between modems and teletypewriters.

Over the years, Java programmers studied the concept behind serial communication. And, as years passed, it was developed; now, the programming language incorporates *java serialization*.

On a related note, other programmers are concerned; since Java is a platform-independent programming language, serialization seems difficult to accomplish. However, while the whole concept of serialization accompanies a string of complications, the task is doable; granted that thorough understanding of serials and serialization is in place.

Chapter Overview

Understanding the Definition of Serials

Understanding the Basics of Serialization

Understanding Transient Fields & Static Fields

Learning the Purpose of Input Streams & Output Streams

Learning How to Transfer Data Safely

What Are Serials?

In the Java universe, *serials* are used to associate an element with another element; the elements in subject include network, databases, and individual files. They are meant to flatten an element and categorize them with other elements in an ordered stream of bytes, and these streams of bytes are, then, set aside to either be used later or modify an existing element. To identify a serialized element, look at its filename; it usually comes with the extension .*ser.*

Serialization may be used for any element; it cannot, however, be used to associate elements that are not compatible with *java.io.externalizable* or *java.io.serializable.* it argues that, although it can accommodate any element, it does not support *static* or *transient* fields.

Transient & Static Fields 101

Transient fields in Java are those that restrict particular elements from being included in a stream, as well as from getting restored due to previous de-serialization. In a way, due to these fields, a Java program can be designed with an ordered structure; random elements, if they remain undeclared, are prevented from being incorporated into a program component.

Moreover, transient fields can be recognized via *transient keywords.* They are known to enter a program by introducing a specific modifier. Since various elements may be in play, a keyword's purpose, in this essence, is to point out a particular element, along with the need for its serialization.

Meanwhile, static fields are those that belong to a class, but not in an instance of that class. They are fields that need meticulous categorization. Usually, they have fixed locations in a program.

Just like transient fields, the purpose of static fields is to set order for a solid program structure. Since both fields are as important as other concepts behind serialization, understanding their relevance is a practical way of successfully understanding serial communication.

Input Streams & Output Streams

For the serialization of an element, 2 codes can be identified by a compiler as high-level streams: (1) *ObjectInputStream* and (2) *ObjectOutputStream.* There is a need for the process since the entry to different elements in lower streams is not allowed without establishing entry in higher streams.

As mentioned, input streams and output streams are high-level streams. Each one is linked to a low-level stream such as *DiskInputStream* and *DiskOutput Stream* for a separate batch of procedures. Thus, these streams are in charge of the overall categorization of all streams.

The Serialization Process

To serialize an element in Java, it is important to note that you'll be converting, then, re-converting data; a lengthy process may be involved. It's a must to fully analyze the elements that you plan on using to not put their integrity at risk; in other programming languages such as *C* and *Pascal*, a programmer is required to work in a separate I/O file for program components that come with serialization processes.

Important reminders:

- Implementations always begin with an introduction of default methods

- Newly serialized elements may be unrecognizable to older serials

- Fully modifying a previously serialized element is not recommended

Step-by-step serialization process:

1. **Enable object serialization by implementing *java. io.serialize.*** This grants permission to serialize an element with another element.

2. **Write an input and output stream.** This allows you to maintain a program's order.

3. **Check the program.** Go over your work to see if errors are preventing its proper execution once it is passed on to a compiler.

Protected Data Transfer with Serialization

With serialization, data transfer is not only more effective, but it also becomes free of possible dangers. If there is a need to access a particular program component that has underwent serialization, it requires the skill of a programmer for de-serialization.

Data transfer, since an ordered structure is involved should be rid of risks; it can affect an entire program if part of it isn't serialized or de-serialized properly. Programmers, especially, are aware of the advantages of protected exchanges. Without the guarantee that a program can retain its quality, chances are, a programmer won't allow the occurrence of any data conversion. This is partly due to the fact that creating serials is not even a difficult task.

CHAPTER 11

How to Use Inheritance

Based on the discussions featured in the previous chapters, you may already be familiar that if all the elements in one class are transferred to another class, the elements are deemed valid. For instance, if all 5 elements of *class A* are transferred and are merged with the other elements of *class B*, the addition to class B will be recognized by a Java program; the elements remain under class A and the particular class is not omitted from the entire program.

Then, it follows that class A is the *original class*, and in this regard, class B is known as the *subclass*. The elements of the first class may have been moved to another class, but their origins can still be traced; they are still under class A.

This relationship between a class and its subclass is called *inheritance*.

Chapter Overview

***Understanding Inheritance**

***Learning about the Transitive Relation of Inheritance**

***Learning How to Use Inheritance to Include Commands**

***Understanding Java Shadowing**

The Concept behind Inheritance

By most books about Java programming, inheritance is defined as the ability of elements to contain common qualities. Alongside, it highlights the fact that the elements can each have unique features; such features are definitive and they make particular elements stand

JAVA

out. To let a class inherit the elements from another class, the words *extends* should be defined. After an access modifier and a class is declared, the word should follow. Sample:

public class extends

Inheritance shows that due to the elements' transfer from a class to another class, particular defining characteristics are transferred to the other elements in a class. This is useful in programming since there are instances when a programmer needs to "borrow" an element from a different so a program can function as desired.

Transitive Relationship Mean?

The inheritance relation between a class and subclass can be described as *transitive.* In programming and mathematics, this means that the relationship can be traced to a partial order, as well as an equivalence order. If a particular group is introduced together with another set of group, it is said that all the elements in all those groups have associations with each other.

Moreover, the transitive nature of the inheritance relationship points out its extensive and inclusive characteristics. It follows 2 concepts: (1) if *class 1 extends to class 2*, the elements in class 1 are included in class 2, and (2) when *class 2 extends to class 3*, the elements in both class 1 and class 2 are included in class 3. Samples:

Sample # 1 (class max1):

```
public class max1 {
    public max1 () {
        system.out.printLn ("A new class max1 is created.");
    }
}
```

Sample # 2 (class max1 extends to max2):

```
public class max1 extends max2 {
    public max1 () {
        system.out.printLn ("A new class max2 is created.");
    }
}
```

Sample # 3 (class max2 extends to max3):

```
public class max2 extends max3 {
    public max2 () {
        system.out.printLn ("A new class max3 is created.");
    }
}
```

In the samples above, it was shown that the class max1 was initially created; it, then, extends to max2 and to max3. It is stated the 3 classes are related and all the elements that are categorized under them have been grouped as 1.

Using Inheritance to Include a Command in another Class

As mentioned earlier, there are instances when a programmer wants to include a particular command to a program component; this is where he can turn to the inheritance feature of a Java program. Instead of having to declare a new command, and modify an entire program, the task can be simplified by using the extend function. Sample:

```
public class max1 extends max2 {

        public max1 () {

                system.out.println ("A new class max2 is created.");

                system.out.println ("open label A");

        }

}
```

In the sample above, due to the fact that *max1 extends to max2*, the max2 command *open label A* becomes a command under class max1.

Java Shadowing

In the Java universe, *shadowing* is described as a kind of inheritance; the technique is to use 2 variables that are named similarly, but within overlapping scopes. It requires a lower variable and a higher variable; 1 variable overlaps the other variable, which causes the elements of that variable to be hidden. For instance, if the lower variable named *theta* overlaps the higher variable named *beta*, it means that the elements of beta are hidden.

Although these *shadowed* elements are hidden, it does not mean that they are not functional. They are hidden for the mere purpose of not having to display its length.

Conclusion

Thank you and congratulations for finishing this book!

I hope you learned enjoyed reading and learned a lot from it!

By now, you should have a firm grasp on how programs are made and how the Java programming language can fulfill vast functions. Keep in mind that you have only scratched the surface. You are now ready to take on more advanced lessons in programming with ease!

Let this book be a reminder to you that Java programming is a more-than-achievable endeavor to you!

Finally, if you enjoyed this book, please take the time to share your thoughts and post a positive review on Amazon. It'd be greatly appreciated!

Thank you and good luck!

Printed in Great Britain
by Amazon